This book is dedicated to Jay Lose and Charles Lose.

Copyright © 2023
Text by Anne Swartz

All Rights Reserved. No part of this book may be reproduced or used in any manner without written permission of the copyright owner except for the use of quotations in a book review.

ISBN: 978-1-960852-15-1 (Paperback)
ISBN: 978-1-960852-16-8 (Ebook)

Published by Aram Samsam Printing

In Tokyo, Snowball the cat woke up and thought, "What adventures will I find today?"

In his garden, he saw bright butterflies dancing. "Look at them flutter!" Snowball laughed.

He found lots of colorful flowers. "So many colors!," Snowball said.

Snowball loved smelling the flowers.
"Mmm!," he purred.

Now, Snowball went into the busy Tokyo streets.

Snowball saw a sleek black cat. "Wow, you're so shiny!," he said.

The black cat walked ahead. Snowball wondered, "Where's it going?"

Snowball followed, curious and excited.

On a hill, the black cat paused and looked around. What did it see?

Snowball waited and watched.

The black cat started moving again.

Snowball said, "Wait for me!"

The black cat was by the sparkling water now.

"I'm coming too!" Snowball meowed, but he had to get wet first.

Up high, the black cat looked at everything. "What a view!"

From another roof, the black cat looked far away. Snowball wondered, "What does the mystery cat see?"

Climbing up to a high wall, Snowball saw the city. "Everything's so tiny!," he laughed.

Like the black cat, Snowball jumped and looked around at the city.

The mystery cat walked on. Snowball wanted to follow along and catch up to the black cat ahead of him.

The mystery cat looked back in Snowball's direction.

Did the mystery cat see Snowball?

Snowball got more excited thinking this time he might catch the shiny black cat.

At first, Snowball moved back and let the mystery cat keep walking. Do you see Snowball on the side of the street?

Then, once he knew the mystery cat saw him, Snowball came closer, and still closer.

They were not quite sure what the other might do.

Much to his surprise, he was right next to the mystery cat! They decided to play.

They climbed high up, playing fun games.

They played chase, leaping, and laughing in the air.

Finally, they stood side by side, two new friends in Tokyo.